A Tiny Beak and Spiky Feathers

Whose little baby are you?

A Tiny Chick

There is a nest inside this old tree.

nest hole

Inside the nest, a tiny, fluffy chick has just **hatched** from its egg.

chick

Who does this little baby belong to?

The tiny chick belongs to a mother and father cockatiel.

mother cockatiel

egg

The mother cockatiel laid five eggs in the nest.

The mother and father take turns to sit on the eggs to keep them warm.

The father bird also looks out for danger.

father cockatiel

Now a chick has hatched from one of the eggs.

The chick begs its mum and dad for food.

beak ⟶

chick

8

The mum and dad
use their beaks to
feed mushy seeds
to the chick.

9

Soon other chicks hatch.

The baby birds are hungry.

four-day-old chick

They wait for their parents
to bring them food.

The father cockatiel is looking for seeds.

11

crest

10-day-old chick

spikes

12

After 10 days, the chick's eyes open.

He has spikes but no feathers.

He has a little **crest** on his head.

crest

feathers

father cockatiel

When the chick is 15 days old tiny feathers grow from the spikes on his body and wings.

15-day-old chick

wing

feathers

mother cockatiel

15

When the chick is four weeks old, his feathers have grown and he can fly.

He flies around looking for seeds to eat.

four-week-old chick

eight-week-old
chick

father
cockatiel

When the chick is eight weeks old,
he is ready to leave his parents and
take care of himself.

When he is six months old,
the cockatiel has yellow
feathers on his head.

six-month-old
cockatiel

18

He lives in a large group of
cockatiels called a **flock**.

19

When he is 18 months old, the cockatiel finds a **mate**.

Now they will have chicks of their own!

male cockatiel

female cockatiel

Glossary

crest
A tuft of feathers, fur or skin on the head of an animal.

flock
A large group of birds of the same kind that fly or live together.

hatched
Broken out of an egg.

mate
An animal's partner with which it has babies.

Cockatiel Quiz

1 How many eggs did the mother cockatiel lay?

2 What food does the chick eat?

3 What does a cockatiel have on its head?

4 How old is the chick when he can take care of himself?

5 What is a big group of birds called?